HAPPY HAMSTER

HAPPY HAMSTER

How Hamsters Influence Champions with Only a Wheel & Cage

Written by Hami Mahani
and Shawn Gaines

gatekeeper press
Columbus, Ohio

HAPPY HAMSTER
How Hamsters Influence Champions
with Only a Wheel & Cage

Published by Gatekeeper Press
2167 Stringtown Rd, Suite 109
Columbus, OH 43123-2989
www.GatekeeperPress.com

Library of Congress Control Number: 2022935513

ISBN (hardcover): 9781662924873
ISBN (paperback): 9781662924880
eISBN: 9781662924897

PREFACE

I could hear the creature on replay in my head just as I began to get into the zone. Those loud squeals and squeaks from the diabolical hamster that could not get its fix of running on some wretched wheel. The thoughts of that wheel tap-danced on every nerve in my body. The sounds still penetrated my ear canals like nails on a chalkboard. They'd kept me up the other day when I was crashing at a buddy's house. They returned to my mind as a random thought and now were all that I could focus on.

I began to pick up speed, and I became oblivious to everything else around me. Just like that night, I heard intermittent pauses, then the horror returned. Where the heck was that thing going? How could it sustain such a fast pace for so long? Why did it keep going back after falling off? Most of all, why was nobody else bothered by it? There is no way I was the only one in that house that heard it. That hamster quickly became the reason for self-evaluation.

Thinking about my friend's pet hamster on that run took me back to a younger Hami. The twelve-year-old Hami that wore the nickname of Hamster as a badge of honor when I first felt like a champion myself. In middle school, I gained the nickname "Hamster" due to my small frame and quickness on the court.

Now, I am not totally sure if being called a hamster is a good thing. It could also have been done out of mockery, since it closely resembles my name.

Nevertheless, I held on to the possibility that my speed and agility reminded them of a rodent. Either way, I embraced the term and wore it as a badge of honor. I could imagine myself standing in my best heroic pose like *He-man* after stopping one of Skeletor's space villains. (Just to show my age, *He-man* was my favorite childhood superhero. He was a real champion.) Anyway, the hamster became an alter ego I was quite proud to own at the time but forgot about for many years.

TABLE OF CONTENTS

INTRODUCTION

Hey! Let me begin with a word of gratitude and say thank you for taking the time to review *Happy Hamster*. I am Hami Mahani, CEO of 6AM RUN,™ a nutrition company that develops products to enhance the performance of endurance athletes. No, don't be worried; this book isn't written to sell you on my product. However, it is written to sell you on the awareness that there is a champion that dwells in all of us. It's true! Therefore, throughout this book, I will address you by your proper title of "champion."

When I call you a champion, I am not only speaking to the current version of yourself, but I am also addressing that part of you that you may or may not be aware exists. I want you to feel empowered to tap into that fight that you have that is just waiting to be released. I want to wake up that lion or lioness that has been dormant. Most of all, I want you to encourage yourself to get in motion.

Happy Hamster all began with a thought. In my mind's eye, I was able to envision how simplistic the hamster is. In thinking of the simplicity of the pet hamster, I realized how overly complex the simple concepts in life are presented to us. However, many of life's issues have simple solutions. That one solution is movement. That's it! The only way to start attacking any issue that you face begins with movement.

Since that's it, we could just say the book is over, right? Thank you so much for reading. That easy? Not really. Moving goes a little deeper than that. It's also an awareness of how and where we move, what our mentality is, and deciding why we are moving. We also have to make a conscious decision to keep moving.

We need to identify ways to unleash the champion that already is inside of you and point you in a direction that will help you avoid unnecessary hurdles. *Happy Hamster* is designed to encourage you to get active and inspire you to climb to new heights that you haven't even imagined yet. Whether this is day one or you are an advanced athlete, this book *will* increase your quality of life if the tools and advice shared are applied. It's all up to you.

Healthy lifestyle is my passion, and I feel it is my calling. As we address physical health, time management, and mental strength, I will refer to running, as I feel it has been the most enjoyable to me. Running has been the tool that I fall back on, not just for physical health, but mental health as well. However, it can easily be substituted with whatever you prefer.

I felt it important to promote the importance of exercise because of the role that it has played in my own personal ups and downs. With the assistance of my coauthor Shawn, I was able to organize my experiences in a tangible way to inspire my fellow champions.

This book was made with you, the champion, in mind. This book should not be looked at as a scientific or promotional reading. Most of the concepts are simply my theories and insight based on my personal observations and forty-two-year journey. By sharing my story, as well as sharing the examples from others, I hope to inspire you to be your own *Happy Hamster*. So let's go, champ.

PART 1

NEWTON'S LAW

A hamster in motion stays in motion.

Movement is essential for quality of life. How things move in nature and how they react to different forces is physics described in the most general of senses. It's hard to think of physics without thinking about the most famous physicist of them all, Sir Isaac Newton. One of Newton's Laws of physics claims that an object in motion stays in motion, at least until there is an opposing force to stop it. In life, we gain momentum when there are other forces that contribute to propel us forward. Conversely, our momentum can be slowed down or halted when things are no longer working in our favor.

When thinking about the caged hamster, I can only imagine two possible factors that would prevent it from running all night. One, it plummets off the wheel like a tumbling stunt double in an action movie, or two, it simply gets tired of running.

The hamster's natural behavior is very similar to that of us humans. Our movements become repetitive, leaving us to run on our own version of a wheel. Now, we as humans may not fall to our doom while being on our wheels in life, but eventually, the shenanigans must come to an end. Whether we choose to get off the wheel, or life chooses for us, things eventually stop. It doesn't matter if we like the wheel or not. There are a wide range of wheels that we get on in life, and we will discuss more of the various wheels throughout this book. We have to, due to the significance that those wheels play in how we live life.

I am no veterinarian or hamster expert, nor do I intend to be. What I do know, based on my own observations, is that hamsters move with a purpose. Maybe it happens, but I have never seen one going for a casual stroll on the wheel. When they get on their wheel, they move with intensity. Moving is programmed into their DNA.

Hamsters are naturally designed to run, but what is their motivation? While in the wild, hamsters are known to run 5k every day looking for food. So survival as their motivation seems appropriate. Similarly to humans, when they no longer remain in motion, they shorten their life span drastically. Hamsters explore all night in search of dinner. So it only seems right that when stuck in a cage, they take to the wheel for extended periods of time. In the wild, a hamster that doesn't move is at risk of becoming a hearty snack for predators that are in motion. It becomes subject to domination by those predators, or even other hamsters that don't settle for stagnation.

Second, a hamster that doesn't move will eventually starve to death. That food isn't going to gather itself, right?

Last, behind door number three, hamsters face the difficulties of developing poor health to the point of expiration, just like you and me. Failure to move causes weight gain, heart conditions, immunity complications, and other systemic failures. The hamster's ability to stay in motion is an overall means to sustaining life.

It is also believed that hamsters run out of pure boredom while in confinement. Being in an unnatural environment, such as a cage, while simultaneously being designed to venture freely affects their mental state. After all, people in prison do things to occupy their time as well. They play cards, get jacked, read, or whatever else they can do to occupy their days. The mind and body have a need to be stimulated, and the two work together to keep the body in motion.

In Haminomics, the parallel between the hamster and human makes tons of sense, because when the body is not in motion, the mind frame changes. Movement adds to mental clarity, and failure to do so limits creativity.

Humans are natural problem solvers, which is why we are the most advanced species on the planet. However, to utilize our creativity, our minds must be in a state to receive and process new information. In America, the status quo is a work schedule from nine to five with weekends off, and at one point, I was the status quo. I noticed that when I stayed at home, I would flop on the couch, binge-watching Netflix. Although my mind was clear of the events of the day, I was no longer moving. The dishes would pile up, and vacuuming became a challenge.

Eventually, I gained a substantial amount of weight and noticed the buttons crying for help when I got dressed for work. That lack of movement made me less productive. In addition, the answer to problem-solving became pro-crastination. That laziness prevented me from stimulating my mind, which eventually affected me physically.

It wasn't until my body got in motion that I noticed a change. Especially on workdays, I woke up earlier to exercise. Logic would say that if I woke up earlier and exerted more energy, I would deplete my reserves. However, nothing was further from the truth. I actually began to feel more energetic. Taking one hour away from my twenty-four-hour day actually made me more productive. It was like taking away time to add more time simultaneously.

Being on the wheel of laziness only made me more lazy. However, my ill-fit-ting clothes motivated me to do something about it. If you are stuck in a pattern of stagnancy, you must find your own motivator. Use that to set a goal to get active until it becomes habitual. When I started my day with exer-cise, I was starting my day with a goal completed before I did anything else.

Studies say that starting your day with exercise can provide you with the same energy as a cup of coffee. Your heart is pumping, and your brain releas-es endorphins to improve your mood. Ultimately, you can respond to situa-tions in a more positive way because you feel good about yourself.

CHAPTER 2

SAME SHIT, DIFFERENT DAY

While considering a hamster running in its cage during a run, I reverted back to the behaviors of a younger adult version of myself. I was a Hami that had turned into Mr. Nine-to-Five. I was simply the hamster running on a wheel to nowhere, only concerned with the redundancy of completing the same day-to-day tasks. Wake up, go to work, do family stuff for a few hours before it was time for bed. Then the next day, wake up, go to work, do family stuff. Then, you guessed it, go to sleep for work, so I could do it all over again. Wash, rinse, and repeat, if you will.

Monday through Friday, with occasional overtime, with one path in mind—just to make it to the weekend so that I could stay in bed until mid-afternoon. Get up just to sit back down on the couch and veg out unless I absolutely had to move. Sprinkle in a little partying and a few hangovers, then, boom, right back to the Monday grind.

I was definitely a caged hamster that was on a wheel. Wheels are designed to propel something, yet my wheel was merely a loop of mediocrity. I was doing the same shit, just on different days.

Take a moment and ask yourself, do you remember what you did last Tuesday? Or what about what you did any given Tuesday three months ago? Maybe it's not Tuesday for you specifically, and there is a random day of the week that you can use instead to personalize the question.

The point is that humans are creatures of habits, whether they are good or bad. We naturally like order and repetition. So if you can tell me what you did on those Tuesdays, your answer will most likely be vague and nondescriptive. You would probably respond with a list of routine tasks, such as: woke up at six, had coffee, went to work, picked the kids up from school, and cooked dinner before going to bed. It doesn't take long before that gets boring, because you do the same exact thing every Tuesday with insignificantly slight variations. Some people are so dependent on that schedule that any change in events can turn their whole day upside down.

Oddly, there are specific dates or moments that occurred five plus years ago that you can go into great detail about. Have you ever wondered why that is? How is it possible that you can be more descriptive about what you did on, let's make up a date, September 22, 2015, than what you did two days ago? This is because on that particular day, you did something outside of the norm. You fell off the wheel for that moment, and it shook up your day-to-day activities. Had it been like every other day, it wouldn't stand out as much, because your schedule is pretty much set on cruise control.

I totally understand and most definitely value schedules and structure. However, mundane tasks don't always work in our favor when we are in the process of growth. Improvement comes with stepping out of our comfort zone and actively seeking ways to make old ways for new adventures. When you are stuck in a loop, then you have to pinpoint where the glitches are. If you are not happy with the wheel that you are on, find another one. Think about it: when you are done with the shower, do you leave the water running just in case you may want to get back in there later? No. What you do is turn the water off and get out so that you can move on to something else.

I have coached youth sports, and there I have seen a tremendous amount of potential in my players. Frequently, kids that are great ball handlers are ecstatic at doing ball-handling drills. The same goes for other skills. My shooters would prefer to shoot threes all practice, and my finishers love doing layups. During the warm-ups, if not guided to do otherwise, the players continuously work on the skills that they are already proficient in. They get comfortable. Resting in their comfort zone allows them to stay deficient in other areas. You can't get better at shooting free throws if you never go to the line.

The lack of confidence in a certain area creates a fear of moving on. Although fear can take on many forms, the fear that I am talking about is cowardliness. You may be CEO material, but if you are staying in a dead-end position, you will never find out. Instead, you will continue to complain about why things are not moving in the direction that you want. If you keep doing the same thing, then you should not be surprised when you get the same results. However, champions can't be afraid to address their weaknesses.

That goes beyond sports, even to how effective you are at work and at home. Champions get off the wheel of fear and get on the wheel of courage. Every day, champions make a conscious decision to capitalize on any opportunity for greatness. Fear is our natural safety net, but sometimes you have to take a risk and have failures that will provide you with real-life learning experiences. Don't cage yourself with so much fear that you lose the ability to thrive.

If you are serious about finally getting into shape, you don't need to wait for a New Year's resolution. Your tomorrow starts today. The things that you decide to do today is the beginning of your journey. Shake it up! Too often, when we decide to change our habits, we fall short. It's okay, though, because that champion still dwells inside you. The cool thing about life is, every second that you are alive is a new opportunity to make a change for the better.

Jump on the wheel of breaking the chain of destructive habits. I know it sounds easier said than done, but running on the wheel of success is a skill. Do not expect to change overnight; instead, make an effort to improve your life. As you continue to practice those skills, you will improve. When you fall off the wheel of improvement, dust yourself off and get your ass back on track. Make it habitual that you won't accept laziness or mediocrity. If you are going to do the same stuff every day, make it count toward something. Going through the motions just to get by will leave you in a position wondering where all of your time went.

CHAPTER 3

THE BIGGER VISION

On a daily stroll, a young woman came across an older gentleman who was digging holes in an empty field. The young woman stopped and curiously asked the gentleman what he was doing. The gentleman politely replied, "I am planting seeds." The two exchanged smiles, and the woman continued her stroll.

Shortly afterward, she met another gentleman on her path who also was digging holes in the ground. She again stopped and asked him what he was doing. The second gentleman looked up and cheerfully replied, "I'm growing vegetables." The young woman grinned and wished him well as she continued her walk.

Moments later, she noticed a third gentleman. She greeted him as she approached him, then once again stopped to ask him what he was doing. The man stood up ecstatically with a smile that stretched across his face. He joyfully replied, "I am making the biggest garden that this town has ever seen.

This garden will be able to feed millions for generations to come."

Champions don't just look at the tasks at hand as something small. They recognize that there is a process to being great, and what they are doing today will affect the end result. When we compare the three gentlemen that were digging holes, you can see how vision separates one from the other, despite the fact that they were all doing the exact same thing. It all begins with a vision. When you think small, then you should expect small results. Conversely, the bigger the vision, the greater the end reward.

What we believe to be true makes a statement true, despite how wrong we are. If I told you I have a new car outside for you, but you don't believe me, then that car doesn't exist, even if you see it with your own eyes. If you don't believe that it is truly yours, then you won't take it. I can give you the keys, the title, and put your name on the license plate. However, nothing that I do will matter because of your disbelief. You need to see your goals and believe that whatever you want is an absolute possibility.

It doesn't matter if other people fail to see your vision, because your vision is designed for your eyes only. There will be people that doubt your vision. However, most won't outright tell you they don't believe in you. Instead, you will get an overwhelming number of opinions on how you should move forward. You'll get offered advice that you never asked for, often from people who actually know very little about the subject. Of course, there's also my favorite "all you gotta do is" person, who just so happens to be someone who has never actually done what you are setting out to accomplish. Sometimes they make valid points that you should consider.

Take all those pointers with discernment. However, too much input turns your dream into someone else's, all because you were too afraid to believe in your abilities and allowed doubt to take over. The wheel of doubt will distance you from your goals before you have even had a chance to start working toward them.

A negative outlook will put a mountain in the middle of an open field. People often say that they want to be happy, but their actions only reflect a negative perspective. Every year, people make statements similar to "There's a bug going around. I'll probably catch it." Or the good old "I always get sick at this time of year." Why is that acceptable, but if a person was to say "I'm healthy and I never get sick," it's unfathomable? That perspective only accepts death and neglects life as a possibility. With the acceptance of the negative, people are guaranteed to get sick.

As a champion, you must exercise humility and expand your thought process to something more positive. I don't care if I'm coughing up a lung, with snot running down my face. I'm not in denial that I have symptoms, but my inner champion is not going to settle for me not feeling well. Instead, we have to envision ourselves feeling better. We have to see ourselves being healthy in a time when it seems impossible to others. You must be selective on who you give permission to influence what you do.

Perception is 100 percent of what reality is made of.

I know you have met a person that has all the answers. Someone who is never wrong, despite their thought process opposing reality. They lack the humility to not be offended when they are corrected. As a result, they stay in the loop of poor arguments and decision-making because of what they perceive. We have to be mindful that we are not that someone. Working within a narrowed perspective is a setup for failure due to the inability to broaden our spectrum.

Thanks to the help of social media, we live in a world full of smoke and mirrors. We are given snippets and a perception that things are what they are. No one has to tell you anything. There is a picture painted, and our mind will fill in the blanks without feeling the need to dig deeper.

People will go on one vacation and post twenty pictures. Others will go to their page and see those same pictures. Then they are given the perception that that person is really enjoying life, ignoring the fact that those same images were taken more than three months ago on the same day. How many are brave enough to show you the ugly, like how they got food poisoning on vacation and vomited on a brand-new outfit that they bought specifically for that trip? How about the part where they left their ID in the car and couldn't board their flight, leading them to have to wait an additional eight hours in the airport next to a screaming baby until the next plane arrived? That's the reality; their whole vacation was not rainbows and unicorns. They had challenges of their own to face. They don't mention the obstacles, but the viewer's mind sees a whole different trip from the one that actually occurred.

The same thing occurs with athletes or people in high positions. You see the championships, the successful business, and the recognition. Those people are champions because of what they were willing to sacrifice to take their visions to the next level. Sometimes you will miss out on parties. Sometimes you will lose sleep. More often than what gets credit, you *will* feel like giving up. Champions didn't get there by accident; they put in countless hours behind the scenes. Many of them are still grinding it out on a daily basis, but the only part that you see is the victory.

Regardless of how you feel, it will be necessary that you continue to visualize and move. When you create your goals, remember that you are on your own time frame. You compete with yourself. You can't see what someone else has done, and think it's going to play out the same for you. Instead, you must give respect to the grind and grind it out for yourself. If someone else has achieved what you are aspiring to have, develop your own path to get it done. One that is designed specifically for *you*.

CHAPTER 4

RUNNING CLOCK

*If time is money, then your health
is your wealth.*

You can always find ways to generate more revenue. Get another job, develop a good or a service. There are plenty who have gone broke and found ways to make it back and sometimes multiply what they previously had. That same idea of "I can get it back" does not apply to time. We can't create more time.

How we spend our time should require just as much consideration as when we make a large purchase. Time should demand your respect. You owe it to yourself to use your time in the most productive manner. Health equates to wealth, and time is money. Therefore, the best way to gain more time is to improve your health.

Making an excuse as to why we cannot do something is always the easy way out. It's a safe bet. There is no way to fail if you never try, right? Wrong. This mentality means that you have already forfeited any potential opportunities because you failed to take on that new challenge.

Have you ever met an "About to?" You know, the people that say stuff like "I was about to run, but..." "I was going to join the military, but..." "I was supposed to start working out, but..." "I wanted to start waking up earlier, but..." But, but, but, but. Well, they might as well be ashtrays; all they ever seem to have is used up butts and plenty of excuses. Sure, in their mind they considered the idea, but in reality, were those people ever really going to do what they said they were going to do?

I get that there was once a goal in mind. However, in most cases, they fall short because they were not as serious about that specific goal as they say. I'm sure in some circumstances there were mitigating factors, but there was no action. That lack of action allowed for the passing of more time, to the point where that dream was nothing more than that. Time continually moves, and your dreams crave to move forward, too!

Let's humble ourselves before pointing fingers, though, because we all have been a Mr. or Ms. About-To at some point in our lives, missing out or delaying an opportunity to become a different version of ourselves. Not getting a chance to add a new experience to the timeline of our life. The good thing is that although we may have missed one opportunity, this doesn't mean that it was our last chance. We may not get the same chance, but new opportunities will arise. When they do arise, we have to remind ourselves that we are not About-To people; we are doers. Champions seek ways to turn "I can't" into "How can I?" whenever they face new challenges. We have to run on the wheel of committing to our goals. Despite the curveballs we face, the new version of you doesn't have the time to remain dormant.

When we receive a gift, it is often hard to accept. We often blush and become speechless, making a statement like, "Oh, you shouldn't have." We have difficulty accepting a nice gesture without having the expectation that we must reciprocate. Meanwhile, when someone owes us, then, out of entitlement, we are not so reluctant to claim what we feel we are owed. Why is that? I believe it is because we have created a defense due to our previous letdowns. Society has caused us to be more receptive and accepting of negativity than accepting of positive feedback. That outlook does nothing for your mental health, and eventually it will affect your physical health as well.

To me, the greatest gifts of all are life and time. However, if we fail to have that outlook, we get caught up in the temporary satisfaction of accumulating stuff, most of which we neither need nor benefit from, outside of the immediate gratification. The memories created with loved ones, the way of new ideas, the success of a business all require time. But in order to give yourself time, you have to be healthy enough to use that time.

What better way to give yourself the best chance at creating more time than by practicing healthy behaviors? You owe it to the future you to develop a lifestyle that will enable you to create cherished moments. Your physical health is one of the few investments that you can make with little to no money and still make exponential gains.

To start running, all you need is the ability and a desire to move. You may have to pay for a pair of appropriate running shoes, but there are even some that prefer to run barefoot. You can do push-ups or crunches, and it will cost you absolutely nothing. Nothing besides time. However, devoting that time to exercise is time well spent. I can't think of any other investment that you can make that will cost you nothing, yet yield a better return on your investment. The time you put in will reward you with the effort that you devote to it.

This simple concept of valuing your health is something that most successful CEOs have in common. It is not a secret that most successful business owners have a regular routine that is committed to their health. Many of them claim that they wake up around 5:00 a.m. daily in order to exercise and get mentally prepared for the day. Getting your day started with exercise is said to provide the same, if not more, energy as starting the day out with coffee. A natural stimulant, if you will.

While exercising is not pure meditation, it is the time allotted to clear your mind and focus on the now, allowing you to actively be present. While you're thinking about getting one more rep out or pushing a little harder on your run, there is no time to focus on anything else.

Can you think of any CEOs who are out of shape? I am sure there are some, but I can't think of any. Could it be that they understand that their health equates to wealth? That time that they commit to a healthy lifestyle prolongs their life, and in return, they are able to make more money. It's hard to run a successful business when you are in and out of a hospital or are unavailable because you are constantly sick.

The clock is ticking, so what you decide to do with the gift of time is of total importance. There are plenty of things to distract you from being productive. I am not suggesting that you give up all of your vices, but if you're going to waste time, then you need to set limitations. Set an alarm before you go down the rabbit hole of clickbait on the web. Create your own limitations and make a plan to stop when the alarm goes off. I don't have to tell you; you already know what's occupying all of your time. Write your plans for the day and check them off as you complete each goal.

Before I go to bed, I am already thinking about what I have to do for the next day. Being proactive in organizing what I'm going to do tomorrow allows me to efficiently use the same twenty-four hours that you have. Most of the day is spent between a combination of sleep and work. If you sleep for eight hours and work for eight hours, then your remaining eight hours need to be utilized as efficiently as possible. If you dedicate only thirty minutes daily to your physical health, then I guarantee a change in your productivity and confidence for every other moment that you are awake.

PART 2

CHAPTER 5

THE HARD WORK DILEMMA

Everyone has a role to play, and some fail to get nearly as much credit as they deserve. A good example is a high school janitor or custodian. Let's call him Joe. Joe is a high school janitor who has busted his tail for many years. Custodians are entrusted with the maintenance and upkeep of the facility. They have to fix stuff, move heavy school equipment, maintain school grounds, and clean vomit, all with little to no recognition.

Joe is practically invisible to everyone. However, if he fails to do his job, then everyone freaks out. It quickly becomes obvious when the trash cans are overfilled, but that same trash can receives no attention when it has a new liner. People just continue to throw things away, while often missing the receptacle without picking up after themselves. Joe routinely picks it up because he takes pride in his work and puts forth his best effort daily because of his own incentive. Daily he returns home sweaty, physically exhausted, and in clothes covered in various unknown stains. We can't deny that our friend Joe is a hard worker.

When you gain respect for time, you look for ways to be more efficient and productive. You have to be that wild hamster that moves with a purpose, getting up and planning your actions with a vision of success in mind. Too often we, with good intentions, look for advice to help us advance on our journey. However, the common saying that we often hear is "You have to work hard" or "Hard work pays." That is pretty much it. Phrases like these are supposed to be used to help motivate us.

Unfortunately, this is often not the answer that we are looking for, and it does not provide even a fraction of information that we need. They are just a cop out, maybe because that person really doesn't have the answers that you are looking for. There is also the possibility that people deem you worthy enough to give away their secrets without receiving something in return. It might even be because all of "their success" directly results from the hard work that others around them have put in, exposing that the one-man band is actually a whole orchestra.

To be honest, I really don't know why *hard work* is the term that people fall back on as a blanket statement. What I do know is that the cliché is a reality. After hearing this term so often, especially when I was in the beginning stages of starting *6AM Run™*, I realized that the term "motivate" usually translates to "deceive." We become deceived in believing that we will have a different outcome when we are on the loop of solely relying on hard work. Well, I no longer want to be motivated. If I'm going to be pushed, I want to be inspired and encouraged and educated on the subject matter. If you ask any successful people, they will have to admit that there was someone or a group of individuals that helped them along the way. Their success wasn't just a result of hard work alone. At some point, there was coaching, emotional support, financial assistance, or some other unsung hero that helped to propel them forward.

Most people aren't business owners, and of the business owners, a lot are still working just as hard to earn a check. Look at Joe. Doesn't he work hard every day? So what happened to all the hard-work-will-get-you-far crap? What is it that makes Joe not nearly as wealthy as CEOs? Oh, could it be that hard-work type of advice is only an illusion that makes people like Joe think they will be rich or at least financially free someday?

After all, Joe "works hard." Not only does Joe work hard, but he has to work more overtime hours to make his paychecks increase. Often the return on that investment ends up being stress, lack of rest, heartburn, and a bad back. Joe misses family functions because he is motivated to just work hard.

The issue has to be deeper than working hard, and we have to work more intentionally to be more effective in our daily life. You need to figure out what you are trying to achieve and work hard at. Picking a direction that you want to go while working hard is what will elevate you. Along the way, there is also networking and continuous education to help you move. There will be valuable jewels that you will learn and apply to all that hard work that you are doing to get you to where you want to be.

When you fail to move without an intended purpose, you are exerting energy to yield minimal results. As a champion, minimal results just ain't going to cut it. The most skilled athletes have trainers to enhance their abilities, but while they are developing, they make sure they are working hard. They are fixing their form and techniques in their off hours and making their success look effortless.

As a champion, you should desire it all and have a desire to max out on whatever life offers, then ask for more. No, you should demand more. More from yourself. Strive for new personal records. Squeeze out one more rep. Go and conquer one more obstacle. The invisible effort becomes visible through your success.

CHAPTER 6

ALMOST ISN'T GOOD ENOUGH

My dad was such a vital component in my life. While I was growing up, this man worked nonstop to ensure that I was taken care of. Coming to America as an immigrant, he learned very quickly what it meant to start from the bottom. It was his influence that molded my personality. His grit and determination created the drive that lies at the foundation of my character.

As a kid, I was maybe a C student at best, and in my mind, a pretty good athlete. Every time I came home from a game, I would be so happy to tell my dad about how well I played. "Hey, Dad, I scored sixteen points" or "Dad, I scored three goals."

Every time he would give me a monotone "good job." Immediately preceding unenthusiastic congratulations, he would follow up with "Did your team win?" or "Did someone score more than you?" Brushing off the questions, I always reverted to the outstanding job that I did on my end. Some would take it as my dad going slightly overboard, maybe even being unsupportive. Well, at least I did, with the thought of, "Why even ask those types of things when I just put on a heck of a show?"

A similar event happened to me when this C student stepped it up academically and got his first B+ on a test. A part of me was reluctant to tell my dad about the best grade of my high school career. A small part of me already knew what to expect. But the feeling of accomplishment overrode that small insecurity. As usual, all proud of my accomplishment, I whipped out the test with the red B+ next to my name. His response became a pivotal moment in my life.

I hope you're not thinking that he said something along the lines of "I'm proud of you." Hell, no. With a typical vanilla demeanor, he said, "That's nice, but, (here we go with the but), was there someone else in the class who got an A?" Immediately, I admitted to him that there was a girl that did. He casually replied, "Your B means shit because you should have been that girl. That A should have been yours." Then he went on to explain to me that there is always someone working harder than you. In order to be great, you have to outwork everyone else.

And just like that, it all made sense. I trusted the opinion of my dad. I knew that he loved me. It was that trust and that love that made me realize he wanted me to be great at everything and never to settle for mediocrity. He wasn't getting on my case about being better for the thrills. He acknowledged that I had untapped potential and there was a champion in me, waiting to be set free. Before this epiphany, I was running on a wheel of just getting by. My average mind operated in defensive mode, because going above par required effort that I was too lazy to give.

I know in the previous chapter, I talked to you about hard work. And this is in no way contradictory to what I said before, because we need to work hard. As previously stated, we don't just work hard, but we work hard with a purpose. The energy that you put toward a particular goal may be the final factor in deciding if you succeed or fail.

We often attack objectives with a half-assed approach, when in reality it is a must that we put our best foot forward into every task that is laid in front of us. There is no settling or just getting by for a champion. Putting in that extra time is going to separate your level of success compared to your counterparts.

Let us not deny the fact that there are some people who are just naturally talented. What they touch turns to gold. But how long can they sustain a level of dominance if they are relying on their natural talent? If they fail to put in the work, then, they will ultimately remain stagnant. While they stagnate, they will slowly see those who are putting in the work surpass their talent. Everyone has their own journey that they have to travel. So if you are not where you want to be at the moment, that doesn't mean that you can't put in the work to get there.

Sometimes we are given things to do that we don't enjoy. No matter how hard or impossible things are, stuff needs to get done. You have to actively seek ways to complete goals, even when you don't feel like it. That feeling is only an emotion, and emotions are a temporary state of mind. Remind yourself of that. A temporary state does not define who you are; it is only a description of what you are going through at the moment. You have to remember that you are not lazy, depressed, or exhausted. Instead, remind yourself during those times, that what you really are is a champion.

You must remember that the real competition is with yourself. Others may be present, and you can use them as an external motivator. However, it all boils down to how hard you are willing to work to ensure that you can persevere.

CHAPTER 7

SPRINT TO A MARATHON

It doesn't matter where you start:
One block, one mile, one marathon.

L et's begin this chapter with two obvious facts. One, sprinters run. Two, marathon runners run as well. No matter how technical you want to be with the terms, there is no denying the fact that they are runners. They both run with a finish line in mind before they begin. There are countless hours dedicated to their craft, preparing them for a race. There are specific diets that contribute to their performance. Overall, they must constantly be in motion to make it to the finish line.

Although they are both runners, the way that sprinters train versus marathon runners differ. The most obvious difference is the distance they run. The time committed to a sprint can be done in seconds. Meanwhile, even the most advanced runners will need hours to complete a marathon. On a more technical view, the running mechanics change based on the distance that people intend to cover. The heel strike and stride change because the body cannot sustain top speeds for extended durations.

Our life is one big race, and within it, we will have various marathons and sprints. These are the long-term and short-term goals we encounter between birth and death. We have the choice to not make a goal, but when we run without a destination, we risk of getting lost. Runners map out their routes; occasionally they veer off course for a little while, but they are aware of where they will start and where they should finish. The same goes for driving a car. You type in a destination on the GPS, and you head in that direction. If there are detours along the way, necessary adjustments are made and you get back on course.

Our sprints and marathons are directly related, whether we acknowledge it or not. We cannot complete our longer goals without completing the short-term goals that precede them. The types of short-term goals we decide to accomplish may determine how our marathon ends. Everything that you do has importance. How you carry yourself, what you think about and when, how you spend your time, your training program. It all matters.

Sprinters's ability to reach top speeds in such a short distance is an amazing skill. When they compete, they give the race everything that they have and leave it all on the track. Although physically drained, they get to the finish line knowing that they have put their best foot forward. As we are working on our own sprints, then you need to carry that same mentality.

When you race, only one person can come in first. I don't care how many participation trophies are handed out; there is always a placement system that identifies who was better than everyone else. There will be people that lose, but that doesn't make them losers because they have had an ability to provide an opportunity for growth. You only truly lose when you give up.

As you set out to accomplish your goals, there will be times when you have not done as well as you wanted to. That is where you need to self-evaluate and see where you went wrong. Begin by asking yourself questions such as the following: Why didn't you do what you set out to accomplish? What adjustments can you make? However, when you do complete your goal, have an understanding that this is not your last race. There is a time to celebrate, but just like the person that came in last, you will have to compete again, even if you are not running in the same race.

When we make goals, there is a process that is involved in getting us to a specific destination. Figuratively speaking, our marathons in life are a compilation of our sprints. If you were to look at them in a literal sense, they would be described as checkpoints. The sprints are extremely valuable because they are the smaller goals that we have to achieve before we get to the end of a marathon. It makes the marathon more manageable. Big goals can be overwhelming, especially in the beginning stages. However, when we decide to break them down into more reasonable goals, something daunting becomes more tolerable.

When people want to lose weight for the first time, going through the process of weight loss becomes a marathon. They start off by saying something like, "I need to lose a given number of pounds in a certain time frame." Great, they know where the finish line is. Once they have made their mind up to proceed, they go with extreme diets or exercising. This is good, too, because they are aware of where to start. However, the problem tends to be those smaller races between the beginning and end; that leads to failure.

It's easy to feel defeated when you feel like there is no progress. They are not seeing the desired progress, not because the intentions are flawed. They are not seeing progress because their vision is too cumbersome. They are only focused on the start and the finish, with little consideration for what needs to go on during the process.

A successful weight loss plan breaks down the monthly goals into day to day, each day having its own specific sprints, and each sprint having its own plan of attack. People's weight loss may not be as fast as someone else's, but it won't matter because they will notice the constant improvement due to their perseverance.

Like I said, everything you do matters. It's similar to a mason laying bricks. He may start off with laying one lonely brick. As he continues to lay bricks, it eventually becomes a wall. After multiple walls have been built, we are left looking at a beautiful castle.

There is a famous program designed for runners called the Couch to 5k. In the beginning, you start off walking. Shortly afterward, you throw in a few minutes of jogging during your walks. By the end of the program, the runner can complete a 5k without stopping for a walk. It uses the same brick-by-brick approach of working smaller and building upon that.

It's as simple as goal by goal, race by race, one moment at a time. You have to focus on the task at hand and realize this is one step closer to excellence. Therefore, give your goals everything that you've got. Don't worry about what you were; visualize who you will be. Embrace the failures, then own them, and learn from them. Sprint with the mind of a champion that is building up toward a marathon.

CHAPTER 8

LIVE LIKE LUKAS

Handsome, smart, courageous, compassionate, and one hell of an athlete, Lukas set foot on the football field at the age of six and quickly earned the nickname of "Dutch Destroyer." Coming from a family of die-hard Philadelphia Eagles fans, Lukas also fell in love with the team, with dreams of eventually playing for the organization. Modeling himself after his two older brothers, Lukas approached the field with a fearlessness and passion for the sport that was hard-wired into his DNA, even helping his team travel out of state for a national championship.

In 2016, at only eight years old, his short-lived football career was forced to be put on hold as Lukas began to complain of stomach pain. His family took him in for an evaluation, anticipating this stomach bug he had would be addressed so that he could return to the gridiron. However, after an X-ray and additional testing, it was revealed that this bug was actually a tumor the size of a grapefruit. Lukas was quickly diagnosed with a rare type of cancer called rhabdomyosarcoma. This led to Lukas being admitted to a hospital, with his mother, Rebecca, never leaving his side.

The next year and a half was quite a setback for Lukas as he spent a large amount of time in a medically induced coma, breathing and being fed via tubes. The tumor would eventually grow into the size of a football, which would lead to Lukas dealing with numerous surgeries, countless allergic reactions, and multiple infections. Lukas spent his ninth birthday in the hospital, surrounded by Rebecca and many other family members. Under this prolonged stress, Rebecca's health was also being put in jeopardy. Fast food, lack of sleep, increased worry, and little to no movement led to Rebecca gaining weight as her own body was a minimal concern while she was attempting to be strong for her son.

A silver lining eventually appeared during this time, as it appeared that the countless treatments were working. Lukas was eventually brought out of his medically induced coma. However, he had to relearn how to walk again at nine years old. Not being able to walk was not going to stop Lukas, as the fighter in him would not allow for him to play victim to any of life's challenges. He made excellent progress, only looking at what was to come in the future. Rebecca's heart filled with hope that this nightmare was now showing signs of being over. Preparations for a celebration of Lukas's return to normalcy became a new focus.

During his journey, it was well known that Lukas was a big Eagles fan. So, one of his radiation technicians reached out to the Eagles organization on Lukas's behalf. During his time in the hospital, Lukas and Rebecca spent a lot of time following the potential drafting of Carson Wentz. They both loved what they saw in Carson, as his smile alone could tell them everything that they needed to know about his character. Shortly after his radiation technician reached out, Lukas received a video message from Carson Wentz. Carson let Lukas know that he was praying for him and wished him the best. That video meant the absolute world to Lukas.

Things looked promising, but once again the pendulum swung. Toward the end of Lukas's treatment plan, the doctors returned to Rebecca with an updated report that the cancer was back and had spread. The doctors offered a treatment plan that would make Lukas even sicker and would require him to be admitted to the hospital. They informed her that this treatment plan would only buy Lukas more time. Despite being so young and having every reason to give up, Lukas continued to fight and be a breath of fresh air to those around him.

When things took a turn for the worst, Lukas's caregivers at the hospital wanted to ensure that he could use his "Wish" for the Make a Wish Foundation. When he asked what he wanted to do, Lukas responded, "I just want to thank Carson."

Wentz and the Philadelphia Eagles came through in a big way. Eight days prior to his tenth birthday, Lukas was invited to come to the Eagles's practice facility to meet Carson, Nick Foles, Coach Pederson, and many other members of the team. What was supposed to be a quick meet and greet tour turned into hours spent with his hero, Carson Wentz. This made a lasting impression on Lukas—the fact that someone that he admired so deeply had the time not only to personalize a video, but also to hang out with him.

Unfortunately, Lukas passed away four days after his birthday. Rebecca was forced to fill a void that had been her entire reason for existence for the previous year and a half. After all the anxiety, stress, and advocating, only to be met with such a devastating loss, Rebecca quickly realized that she had to find a way to work through the horrendous grief and pain that she was feeling in order to survive. Although her heart was in pieces, she decided to do something about her mental and physical condition. There were other people that still relied on her. So, with that same drive that Lukas had, she looked for a way to change what she could. She opted to make herself a priority and focus on changing her health.

Rebecca began exercising and noted that exercise played a huge role in saving her life. She slowly began with running, then eventually became more focused on lifting weights. Exercise and her time in the gym became her escape from the pressures of the world. While exercising, Rebecca was able to silence all the noise of the world and release tension in a positive way. Jogging on the treadmill provided her with a mental clarity that offered a new way to connect to Lukas. She could hear Lukas's voice and have conversations with him while also receiving words of encouragement.

Needless to say, Rebecca's health improved, although the grieving process never ends. ESPN aired a special highlighting Carson and Lukas's time together, in addition to raising awareness of Lukas's battle with childhood cancer. Shortly after, other families contacted Rebecca to offer support and thank her for sharing her story. She reflected on all the support that she received while she was in the hospital and decided to not only look for ways to change her life, but others as well.

Rebecca started Live Like Lukas, an organization that helps to support other families by letting them know that they are not alone in their battle. Live Like Lucas provides financial support to families with children who are fighting childhood cancer, while simultaneously using raised proceeds to support the fight against childhood cancer.

Hardships and adversities are a normal process in life. There will be times when you feel like you have everything under control, then other times you may not feel so sure. It's okay. When unexpected challenges are thrown your way, that's when it's most critical to allow your inner champion to dominate your mind. It needs to be so dominant that you refuse to quit. Most of the storms that we face will not get better by avoiding them. More than likely, avoidance will only prolong the process. You must come to a point when you have to look at yourself in the mirror and take a firm stand on who you are: a champion. Make a commitment to yourself to be victorious and not a victim. After you recognize who you are, then put things in action to face your problems.

Rebecca had no idea that a minor stomach bug would turn into a life-altering event. Do you think she wanted to be at the hospital with Lukas in that position while still having to work and be a mother to Lukas's brothers, as well as acting as an advocate for her youngest's care? Highly doubtful. If anyone needed someone to help carry a load, Rebecca for sure did. Despite who or what was to blame, both she and Lukas saw that mountain placed in front of them and attacked it. They took on the task of finding a solution by fighting back against adversity.

The recounting of Lukas and Rebecca's events touched me so deeply that my eyes watered. Telling their story is not for anyone to compare their adversities to, but to encourage you to think about your own. We can't compare our hurts to other people's because we have our own journey. Do not allow anyone to downplay your hurt because if it matters to you, then it matters.

It is not for me or anyone else to gauge the severity of your life's challenges. However, we have to evaluate and oppose amplifying things that don't really have a large impact on our lives.

Most of our daily issues are so minute, it's not worth the time that we commit to them. Are the hardships that you are dealing with now really worth all of the energy that you give them? That person driving in the right lane with the blinker on for a quarter mile probably didn't mean to cut you off. So should you really sweat it and allow it to linger? Should every relationship that you encounter have to suffer because of a hurt that was a part of your past that you haven't dealt with?

Sometimes you mess up, but don't we all fall short from time to time? Sometimes other people make mistakes too. In the journey of life, sometimes shit just happens. That's the way the dice fall. We may be left to deal with a problem that we have absolutely no control over. Regardless of what caused the adversity, the ball is in your court. Who gives a damn who is to blame for what happened?

When a problem is presented, what you decide to do next is vital. I do not care if it is the right decision or the wrong decision. What is important is that you make one. Failure to do so will allow life to make a decision for you, and there is a high probability that you won't be satisfied with the outcome. Stop playing the game of chance and start working toward a better you.

The blame game is only used by players with weak minds. Minds that don't understand responsibility. The blame game seeks sympathy instead of solutions. Even though you may not have control over what challenges arise, you still have to learn the importance of taking responsibility for how *you* react to challenges. Adversities suck, but they do not always have to be viewed as all bad. After all, some of the greatest feats of excellence occur when pressure is applied. Challenges can help to elevate you to greater levels. Therefore, by not accepting a challenge, you limit your own potential.

We should be willing to accept challenges and not cower in fear of failure. Use your better judgment when you take on new challenges. I am not insinuating that you should put yourself in harm's way just to prove that you can accomplish something. However, if it is a situation that gets better from then, go toe to toe with it.

It is a natural thing to let negative things fester, sometimes controlling our minds for so long that we may even forget what we were even worried or upset about in the first place. Ultimately, it smothers the mind with a cascade of negative thoughts, leading to a change in our actions. We become short tempered with our coworkers or family members, when in actuality the person that you are really upset with is long removed from the situation. You know, like when that waiter takes too long with the food at breakfast. There may have even been something deviating in your childhood that traumatized you. No matter the circumstance, you have to make a convincing effort to let go of what is not important.

The full emotions may be a natural response, but you have to give yourself a time limit for how long you will allow negativity to visit your mind. If you don't, negativity will live in you rent-free. Practicing forgiveness and patience does not make you weak; it makes room for your mind to focus on the necessary. You don't forgive people to help them; you do it to help you move on with your life. So that *you* can focus on *you* and not fall off your wheel of greatness.

CHAPTER 9

CHEERING FANS

*Don't worry about
who's not clapping in the front row,
because you have a balcony full of people
that want to see you be great.*

It is my personal belief that everyone has their own agenda. I don't mind that at all, because we all should have something that we are chasing after. However, if others's agendas do not align with your own, then it's time to move on. Find someone else that can meet you in agreement, because not having the same agenda will only hinder you on your path. When the members involved cannot agree on what the bigger vision is, then it will ultimately lead to a stalemate. Nobody will benefit, because all the energy that should be used to get to the finish line is spent on dead ends and unnecessary challenges. There is nothing wrong with cutting ties; sometimes that is the one thing that can save positive relationships.

By agenda, I strictly mean goals, which should not be confused with perspectives or methodologies. Often, having a different approach to a situation may lead to an increase of the speed at which we obtained the goal. Sometimes we need to shake things up a little. Be mindful that just because you think you have an answer doesn't mean you have every answer. Being pushed out of your comfort zone stimulates creative ways of solving problems. People that want to see you win, only want to support you. They are often willing to play any role that you give them. However, due to their passion for you, they may overstep the boundaries that you have given them. Instead of going on defense, be grateful that they are in your corner.

Although at times they may seem overly critical, your legit fans have good intentions. They genuinely care about the outcome of your journey. I believe that most people are good, and there aren't very many people that are purely evil. However, some concepts that they push on others are misinformed. Somewhere along the timeline of their lives, their dreams may have been crushed. In return, they unknowingly push that same energy on others. In an attempt to offer help, they can only offer doubt. Certain points of view have been ingrained into them, and they haven't acknowledged that their behaviors are counterproductive. That doesn't necessarily make them bad people, just the wrong people to pursue your dreams with.

Don't spend time allowing any negativity to affect your goal. Instead, be grateful for the fact that they want to support you while acknowledging that they are not mentally ready to. Champions do not allow the ideas of others to deter them from their finish line. Instead, they seek intrinsic motivators to keep pressing on when others can't see what they envision. Champions know that too many opinions will turn their vision into someone else's. Everyone is entitled to have an opinion, but only you have the right to endorse or reject that opinion.

Sometimes those harsh truths are what we need, because there is a lack of self-motivation. When I played basketball, my coach would make us run suicides when someone messed up on a play. I often thought he was just a bitter man who found pleasure in watching us suffer. I saw him later in life and reminisced for a moment about his brutal practices. His response was, "My job was to guide you, not be your friend."

Those words really resonated, because as I recalled, we definitely learned the plays out of fear we would be dying on the baseline. However, if it had been left to us, I do not know if we would have had the motivation to improve our ball IQ ourselves. Not to mention, it improved our weaker teammates's conditioning. As a team, we had one agenda, and that was to win games. And that coach was willing to give it his all to give us the best chance at success.

Not all of your fans will be on the forefront. There are eyes lurking in places that you may forget about. People that want absolutely nothing from you but an opportunity to spectate. They may have only interacted with you one time for a few brief moments, but there was something about your existence that made a lasting impression on them. It could be the random kid who you helped fix a broken chain on his bicycle. Possibly even the cashier you give a genuine smile to when you go to get your morning coffee.

We don't know what other people are going through. Therefore, those seemingly insignificant interactions with you may be what helped someone else get through a challenging day. We may not have the opportunity to acknowledge the people that are looking up to us. But you are not invisible, even if you feel that you are. You are someone else's reason for working harder or feeling empowered. Your secret fan club is rooting for you to be your best, because you are an inspiration.

Coaches and parents and friends can't be with us every moment of the day. There are times when we have to reach deep to get our butts in motion. In order to get in motion, we have to find a reason to do it. Figure out why you do what you do. Then get in motion to actively place yourself in positions that will give you the best chance at success. Let go of insecurities and give yourself the credit that you deserve. But most importantly, you have to be the president of your own fan club.

PART 3

FINISH LINE

When you think
your car is empty, there are still
more fumes left in the tank
to keep you going.

Even though we still have a little further to go in the book, I think it's about time that we introduce the finish line. When we think about the finish line, the term is associated with an ending. The point where we have already run the race, and now we get an opportunity to relax. But that is not how I view finish lines at all. Hear me out on this, and this may sound a bit of an oxymoron, but the finish line is where it all starts over. It doesn't stop at the finish line. Once you have made it that far, it's time to reevaluate and figure out what adjustments need to be made to take things to the next level.

A buddy of mine, who is not a runner, decided to get on the train and start a regular jogging routine. He complained he was out of shape and it was time that he made some adjustments, starting with daily exercise. He set a goal of doing two miles in twelve minutes. In his mind, he used to run six-minute miles, despite it being over eight years since he had last run. Unfortunately, due to his level of fitness, those two miles quickly turned into just wanting to do one mile.

At about the ten-minute mark, he began wheezing and panting. Completing one mile at this point was starting to look like a fantasy as his calves were on fire, and his thighs began cramping.

Trying his best to fight through the fatigue, he tapped out. He said forget this; it's just day one. He was willing to settle for walking the rest of the quarter mile that he had left. After all, due to moving at such a slow pace, the chances of him meeting his initial goal of two miles in twelve minutes were long gone.

He had finally arrived at a point where his heart was pounding, and the only thing that he could focus on was just trying to stay alive. As he came to a complete halt on his course, a deer jumped out of the bushes and darted off five yards in front of him. Equally startled, if not more, my buddy sprinted for an additional two minutes. With his adrenaline pumping, he did not make the time, nor did he get to two miles that day. However, he did run a mile and a half in under fifteen minutes. Tapping into a reserve that he wasn't aware of, he was able to push further than he thought he was capable.

Notice how when my friend made a decision to say, "I'm done with running for today," he was willing to give up on his goal. At that moment, the level of challenge took a stronghold on his mind. He had more left in the tank, but had it not been for that close encounter with a deer, he would not have realized that he had more to give. There is uncharted territory when we allow our minds to give up too soon in our paths.

Much like the hamster, we are designed to keep going. Everyone faces obstacles and walls. However, incorporating the behavior of a champion requires us to keep pushing along. Have you ever noticed how bodybuilders seem to always find something on their body that they need to improve on? To the average person, it seems like bodybuilders's physique looks amazing. However, bodybuilders will look at their body and say, "One thing looks good, but how can I make it better?" They go through rigorous training and meals, and switching out routines in order to make their physiques as perfect as they can before a competition. They see what can be and don't just stop at what's good enough. You have to look at the place that you finish and make a determination of whether you are at the finish line or a temporary rest stop.

January 21, 2017, was my finish line. This is a special date that I hold near and dear to my heart, because Mr. Nine-to-Five was killing it with the sales at a startup. I was working at a tire e-commerce company and was hired to head up their sales and marketing. During my second year there, I negotiated a major deal that would take that company to the next level. This partnership that I negotiated with one of the world's largest retailers generated two hundred million dollars in sales. I felt unstoppable.

Although I was not totally satisfied with my day-to-day life, that moment put me on a major high. I thought this was it. This was it. I had finally made a move that could not only change my life but would positively impact my family forever. Then I got the call into the owner's office. At this point, I was very content with my performance at my job, and this was the conversation that I had been waiting for. Maybe I'd ask for a 10 percent raise. Nah, this was way bigger than a measly 10 percent. No, I'd have my own office, with a good view. I could see myself with my feet propped up while my secretary answered, "Sorry, Mr. Mahani is in a meeting. Can I take a message?"

Since I viewed myself a stellar employee, a call to the office was nothing alarming to me, so I confidently walked into the office, awaiting my praises. "Have a seat, Hami," the owner said to me. "You have been performing very well, and we want to thank you so much. When you were hired, we never thought that you would have been here so soon."

In my mind, I knew that I was darn good at my job, but I remained humble and allowed him the opportunity to shower me with accolades. I just knew he was about to offer me a raise. I had been over the monologue in my head many times. I was going to negotiate and tell him that wasn't enough in case he tried to underplay my contributions.

He continued, "With that said," he paused as I eagerly awaited. "We can't seem to figure out what the best commission is on such a huge number." This was my moment. He finished the sentence with, "So we must let you go. We truly appreciate *everything* you have done and will give you eight weeks' compensation."

Holy crap, that went south quickly and wiped that silly grin off my face. My mind could not fathom what I just heard. *What?* Eight weeks? Eight weeks' compensation for two hundred million in sales. That was only 2 percent; I mean, the average compensation was 3 percent, so you could imagine my frustration. So in addition to being terminated for doing such a good job, they decided to put a cherry on top by low balling me on what I was compensated for.

At this point, I felt like my life was over. I was thinking I, like most people, had other people depending on me. An eight-year-old doesn't want to hear a sob story when he is hungry. I had to make an adjustment because I had just fallen off the hamster wheel that I had gotten so comfortable on.

It was quite the predicament, being that I had financial obligations—family, rent, not to mention my love for sneakers. I was well aware that a change had to be made. It was a sink or swim situation. While clearing my mind on a run, I thought about my body and what it needed as an athlete, and the early stages of 6AM RUN™ became a new focus.

Much like Rebecca, I faced an adversity that seemed like the end for me. However, I had to push forward. Many of us come to a point in our life where we plateau, and that hamster is comfortable enough to keep running on that wheel.

Being forced off the wheel put me into a position to find a new and improved wheel. A wheel where I was able to evaluate the things I hated about the other one and decide to refuse a return to that same insanity. I decided that I would work for myself. In the workforce, they proved how disposable I was. However, if I worked for myself, I could take more control over how my time was spent and who I answered to.

I was preparing to start a brand-new race. One that I created. One where I got to have input on how long it should last and where it ended.

That's it. You need to take control. Take control of your mind. Take control of your health. I'm not saying that everyone should start their own business, but what you need to do is make a decision and stand on it and take owner-ship of whatever you can in life. Your adversities may not be hard to someone else, but they are hard for you. Regardless of how hard things get, you can make a decision to keep going.

CHAPTER 11

RUNNING ROB

"There is no lid on my box of life"
—*Rob Ridgeway*

I met Rob a while back, and we have stayed in contact ever since. Rob is a Marine Corps vet, and even prior to the military, he was always looking for the big "what's next." When deciding what branch to join, he sought the job and the branch that he felt would be the most challenging. During his time in the military, he learned how to take his drive to another level via structure and rigorous training. Rob learned that every challenge is mental, and if you can control the mental, then your body can accomplish just about anything.

Although Rob ran in the military for physical readiness, he never classified himself as being a runner until later in life. Rob's running career began in 2014 when he began doing local charity 5Ks with friends. While Rob did not immediately love the act of running, he loved the atmosphere, comradery, and competition that comes with the sport. Rob began participating in more

5Ks and joined a local running group. It was through this group that Rob's love of running and drive to achieve more really took off.

One day in 2017, the organizer of an upcoming half-marathon showed Rob the finisher's medal for that race. Rob immediately wanted to do whatever it took to get that medal, and, with that, he was now a runner. After completing his first half-marathon and winning numerous awards in his 5K runs, Rob began looking for his next challenge. Enter the Marine Corps Marathon. As a Marine himself, Rob was drawn to the race for what it stood for and decided that it was the perfect first marathon in 2018. Following this, Rob could not be stopped and, in the years that followed, completed more half-marathons around the country, with the goal of completing one in every state. He also finished his first 50K and completed two 50-mile races. Rob's next challenge and goal is to complete his first ever 100 miler in 2022.

Looking at his record of numerous races, Rob still says, "I hate running, but it's all about accomplishing the goals." There is always the "what can I accomplish next" mentality with Rob, and not just when it comes to running. This desire to set and accomplish goals is something that Rob applies to everything in life, from work to home improvements to his family. Everything is all about setting goals and pushing the envelope to see how far he can go.

* * *

Champions thrive when they are on a wheel of goal setting. Often, nobody gives them goals; they hunt them down. Rob is a great example of this; it would have been easy for him to stop at 5Ks with his friends, but he saw more for himself and set his sights on reaching his goals. In about five years, Rob went from not running at all to preparing for a 100-mile race. He wanted, and still wants, that adrenaline rush that comes with doing more.

A mindset of scarcity says that there is not enough to go around. It creates envy and hatred for what others have accomplished, because subconsciously that mind does not believe that it can accomplish the same feats. However, champions like Rob live their lives with an expectation of abundance. There is always more to be had and accomplished. There is more than enough room in this world to succeed, despite how many others have succeeded in the same area. There is no obstacle too big to be tackled.

CHAPTER 12

THE SPOILED BRAT

I don't care what I have to do to get it.
I want what I want.

I am an only child. My father worked multiple jobs in order to give me whatever I wanted. Maybe I got what I wanted because my parents believed that I was lonely. There is also the possibility I deserved my gifts because I was that awesome of a kid. The why really made no difference to me; I just didn't want the gifts to stop. I was not acquainted with the word "no," because my parents always told me yes. Now, they didn't allow me to do anything that would put me in danger. They also taught me to have respect and do things with honor. Nonetheless, the majority of the time, I was able to have my way. After all, not having siblings and being the only grandchild put me in a position to have the world at my fingertips. Needless to say, I was spoiled. I wouldn't consider myself to be a brat, but I definitely acknowledge and am very appreciative that I was never without.

There is often a stigma put on people being spoiled. The outlook is that the spoiled child never learns what it means to be without. If spoiled children don't get their way, they will often throw tantrums, demanding that their orders are fulfilled. They are not accustomed to the word "no." Since "no" is not a part of their vocabulary, it doesn't register when they are told what they cannot have. Being spoiled doesn't teach the importance of hard work, and they are selfish.

There is often some validity to these accusations. However, to some degree, I feel like those types of characteristics can be looked at differently. Getting what you want has a flip side. Those children make a decision and learn to stand firm on their wants. They want what they want, and it doesn't matter how they get it, as long as they get it. With maturity, though, throwing fits when you don't get your way won't fly. It's inappropriate to throw a fit, but the same intensity for getting what you want should still be there. You must learn to turn that tantrum into drive.

To be spoiled doesn't mean that you neglect practicing humility and taking on responsibility. So in no way am I suggesting that you go out and just be the biggest asshole that you can. Nor am I encouraging you to let your pride be a reason for negatively manipulating others for your personal gain. What I want you to see is that being spoiled has the ability to put your mind in a place to think that nothing is unachievable.

A common saying is that the sky's the limit. Well, to be a spoiled brat, you acknowledge that saying still comes with a limitation. Saying that the sky's the limit still establishes a boundary, because when you get to the sky, that's the end.

In high school, I had a teacher who discussed his childhood dreams of being in the NBA. He explained how his lack of height and skill level made him good enough to move on after high school basketball. Despite how hard he worked, he lacked enough talent to be good competition. He couldn't jump high. He wasn't fast. He was a par-level ball handler. He was short. Overall, hard work and passion just weren't enough to allow him to play at the next level. He never stopped loving the game and was determined to get on the court, even after his high school career ended. Eventually he decided to become a referee. Kind of ironic that the kid who could barely get on the floor was now the one who was on the floor for every play.

Well beyond his prime, he was still refereeing games, even though he was sometimes more than twenty years older than everyone else. Where life put up roadblocks, he looked for a way to be a part of what he enjoyed. He didn't make excuses; instead, he developed a solution. That's what champions do. He displayed the qualities of that spoiled brat that wouldn't take no for an answer when it came to growing up and getting more time on the court.

With knowing the determination that he had, if I was able to go back in time, I would have encouraged him to be more specific about what he wanted, informing him that a spoiled brat would be more specific in knowing exactly what they want. Don't just demand to be on the court; demand to be on the court as a player. If he had been more specific in his goal, his basketball career might have been more prolonged. However, since all he wanted was just to be on the court, that's exactly what he got.

You can do the same with your goals too. First you figure out exactly what it is that you want. Then you take your vision and demand that it comes to fruition. After all, what you can't do is not a part of a spoiled persona.

The idea of the spoiled brat being selfish also has a positive twist. There are times when we absolutely need to be selfish in order to keep our inner peace. Selfishness is simply putting yourself and your goals on the top of *your* priority list. You know that six-pack you want or that race you desire to complete next month? Well, it's going to require you to be more selfish with your time. If you aren't being selfish with your time, how do you expect to get to where you want to be? Time is money, and you need to ensure that you are paying yourself first.

Sharing is caring, right? Children are taught at a very young age they are supposed to share with others. They are taught that it's a quality that makes someone a good adult. No doubt, sharing is a great attribute, as long as it is something that you can afford to sacrifice. My wife taught me that if you can't afford to give something away, then you shouldn't let others borrow it. Allowing this to guide the way I give has made things so much smoother in my life. It has given me the ability to gauge boundaries.

When you don't draw a line in the sand, sharing becomes exhausting. Naturally, some people are givers, while others are takers. The difference is takers have no boundaries. Therefore, givers have to set boundaries or else they will put themselves in a position where they are unable to keep giving.

Most of us have been in the position where a relationship is ruined because someone "borrowed" and never paid their debt. The debt doesn't have to even be financial. Maybe someone borrowed your favorite shirt. You go to wear it, and boom! It's not there. How much energy do you give to that? That frustration leads to anger, even if it is momentary. This is energy that would be much better used in other areas. You get in a loop of negativity. Rejecting the inner spoiled child you need to be, you open yourself up to staying on the wheel for an extended period. You knew that you weren't ready to part with that shirt, so why didn't you say no?

Believe it or not, saying "no" is actually a skill, especially when you have a giving heart. Saying "no" requires courage. Declining the offer to go out when you know that you have to be up early can be hard. But in the future you will thank yourself for making that sacrifice, for saying no to things that are not helping you reach your goal. By being selfish with your emotions and not giving the world your time, you are keeping yourself in a position to stay out of cages of the ordinary. You know, deep down inside, what you need to do, and where you want to be, so make a habit of saying no for your own health.

CHAPTER 13

BE YOUR OWN BEST FRIEND

Who is the one friend or family member that you talk to the most on a daily basis? If the answer was anyone other than you, then you answered the question wrong. That one person who you interact with the most in a twenty-four-hour day is yourself. Think about all the internal monologues that you have. You ask yourself questions, then answer them. You evaluate and create hypothetical scenarios in your head. Random thoughts happen, sometimes occurring when you are involved in an actual conversation with someone else.

Your past experiences, influences, and conditioning help you formulate your own opinions. I'm aware that you don't always rely on yourself; sometimes you need a third party for a different perspective prior to decision-making. Maybe you are unsure about some things, and you may seek validation in other areas. People make suggestions as to what you should do next or what you should think. Regardless of the outside sources, you are ultimately the one who decides what you do.

Your choices may also be influenced by a risk-to-benefit analysis that will have you conclude that the consequences are worth the action. You may not weigh the long-term effects in response to seeking immediate gratification because at that moment, that temporary satisfaction appears to be worth the risk. Even if it's not right based on other's standards, you want to do what you feel at that moment is in your own best interest, only you are going to have to justify within yourself why particular actions are appropriate.

Whenever it is possible, good decision-making should be done, with more than immediate satisfaction at play. Consider how your actions today will affect others around you. Most of all, consider how those decisions made will affect you and your journey, like spending your money on an expensive vacation when you know that you are delinquent on your car note. At the time, I'm sure you could justify that decision with a YOLO mentality. But, in the future, you have to suffer from the choices that you made when your car becomes repossessed.

True friends are defined by their actions, and they genuinely care about what happens to other friends. You must start being friends with the future you. Show the future you how much you care about him or her by doing your best to ensure that the later version of yourself can reap the benefits of all the efforts that you put in today.

Think about what you are saying to yourself. Are the conversations that you are having with yourself promoting your value? Are you convincing yourself that you are worth it or worthless? While you are talking to yourself, you should be your biggest cheerleader.

Good cheer teams don't wait until you are winning to keep you encouraged. They start cheering as soon as the game starts, sometimes offering positive energy prior to the game even begins. When the game is close or the home team is down, they are still cheering with a smile, doing what they can to inspire you to rise to the occasion. If a team has a losing season, the cheerleaders will still show up to every game, expecting only the best for their team.

The only downfall of the cheerleaders is they are only available to inspire you for the moment. When you become your own cheerleader, the game is never over. You must constantly root for yourself to come out on top of any situation. You have to love yourself enough to want to change the trajectory of your life and do things that will improve its quality.

It doesn't matter if you are a CEO, custodian, or a student. It doesn't matter if you are financially stable or dirt poor. They are all titles. Titles that identify you as a temporary status that can change at any moment. Once you strip those titles away, you are you. No title will change who you are on the inside. Moving to a different location or winning the lottery may provide you with a momentary satisfaction. However, when the thrill is gone, you are back to dealing with that you.

We can all agree that there is the seen and the unseen. The tangible and intangible. Without getting religious, there is the natural and the supernatural. Nature is where all those titles have a home. However, it is the supernatural where we have to face what is not tangible. Others may not see depression or anxiety. Instead, what is seen is the outcome from the battles of those conditions.

Your mind is constantly at war, telling you what is and is not true. As a result, your perspective affects your decision-making, which affects your actions.

Be aware of the war, and take note of the opposing forces that want to rob you of your peace. You choose what side you want to be on.

There will be times you will need to take a break. But taking the time to gather your footing doesn't mean quitting. You need to have periods where you can regroup to come up with a plan of action that will keep you on your wheel of success. Proper rest is just as important for you physically as it is mentally.

Even the greatest of athletes need rest. Rest to them may not mean sleeping in while time elapses. However, they will have days when they run at a slower pace, do fewer reps, or just dedicate time to rehabilitating a nagging injury. They haven't given up. Instead, they are taking actions to ensure longevity.

You have to be self-aware of when you are turning your time-out into a camp-site. Doing things like losing hours scrolling on social media, eating like crap, or being inactive steals away from things that you could be doing to improve your quality of life. They may feel good at the moment, but the compilation of those habits will require a detox to get you moving in the right direction.

The same concept works for your mind. Overthinking, as well as under-stimulation, needs to have a break in the loop. It's about finding a balance. The inability of trying to find that balance forces your body to call a natural time-out for you via injuries and illness. The mind and the body are directly correlated in the overall picture in terms of your health and productivity. Take a moment to remind yourself of what you need to be doing. When you feel bogged down by the large amounts of decisions, take a time-out and remind yourself that you are a champion.

CONCLUSION

I want to thank you for reading this. If you made it to this section that means so much, and I truly hope whatever victory you are chasing now seems within an easier reach.

If this is your first "Self Help" book, or multiple, I am confident the "First Step" and priority each day MUST be taking care of your PHYSICAL FITNESS. If you can't take care of yourself first, you can NOT and will not be your best self. You can not be the best son or daughter, the best husband or wife, the best Father or Mother, and especially the BEST in any profession you choose in your career. The effects of being your healthiest are BOTH mental, and physical.

Do you see a common theme here? Each and every one of these is that various forms of daily activity and movement will help you get on track to reaching that champion inside yourself.

Maybe the things said may not have changed anything for you because you already have the answers. It's okay if this book is not tailored for you at this moment. However, I do sincerely hope that you have been able to change your perspective on at least one new idea. At a minimum, my desire is to ensure that you have been able to stimulate the knowledge that you already have. If that is this case, then I consider this book to be an absolute win, regardless of any other opinion to the contrary.

While speaking to you, I was also able to speak to myself by reflecting on past experiences and knowledge that I have learned during my journey. This book isn't all-inclusive. There is so much that I haven't spoken on, and that I, too, have yet to get a grasp on. But, as you close this book, I want you to keep in mind that every idea conveyed to you is a skill. A skill that will only get better if you have a desire to put in the work. Desire is the key.

Don't just wish for your lucky break; start preparing for your opportunity. Maybe you don't have the time to fondle the pages to go back to concepts that hit you home. Therefore, I have created a quick guide for you to skip so that you can just jump to the back of the book for a refresher on some of the key concepts.

- A body IN Motion STAYS IN Motion.
- Don't just move, but move with a purpose. See the vision, then make a game plan to execute.
- Give time the respect it deserves.
- Be your own best friend.
- The theme among champions is a SELF desire for more. How bad do YOU want it?

THANK YOU...

While 6AMRun.com and "Happy Hamster" are my vision, and my thoughts on how to be successful in all aspects, it would NOT exist without some amazing people around me.

First my Wife, Best Friend and Life Partner of over 10+ years. Hitomi Rose Mahani, she gambled our entire future and safety net because she believed in me when no one else would. She pushes me to be my BEST every day!

My oldest firstborn daughter, Layla Rose Mahani. She will never know how much impact she has on me. She makes me want to be the best dad, and I will always be there for her! I am so proud of her every day, so her being proud of me means more than anything. This child is my mini me and will one day soon run laps around my accomplishments.

Our youngest, Londyn Skye Mahani... Londyn is a child I do not worry about. She lights up a room just by walking in it, and grew up in the 6AM Run warehouse. She will no doubt one day help people around her shine too! There is not a car ride where she sees a runner outside on the side of the road running, and doesn't scream "6AM Run Try It!"

My Parents. Mariam Saleh and Parviz Mahani. I am who I am because of them. They never allowed me to feel as if I wasn't good enough. My father is my HERO! Every day, my Father puts his needs second to mine, and now the girls. He works here in the 6AM Warehouse, and only out of the JOY of helping us. He never once asks for ANYTHING, just our happiness.

To my friends, business partners, 6AM Run TEAM, Staff, and those who helped 6AMRun.com get here, THANK YOU TOO!

Finally, every Teacher, Coach, and Former Boss who doubted, failed, cut or fired me. I would NOT be here today without you. At those moments I was always so hurt and wondered why I wasn't good enough. Now I know, I was simply being prepared and learning what I needed to possess to survive NOW!

Thank you!
Hami

CPSIA information can be obtained
at www.ICGtesting.com
Printed in the USA
JSHW011525030722
27712JS00001BA/31